STARS

by Lauri Kubuitsile

T0384559

The Sky at Night

We can see the moon
and the stars at night.

The sky is full of stars.

What is a Star?

Stars are made of **dust** and **gas**.

Stars look small but they are big.

They are far away.

FACT A star is a ball of hot gases.

The Sun

The sun is a star.

It looks big because it is close to the **Earth**.

FACT The sun is made of dust and gas too.

Red Dwarf Stars

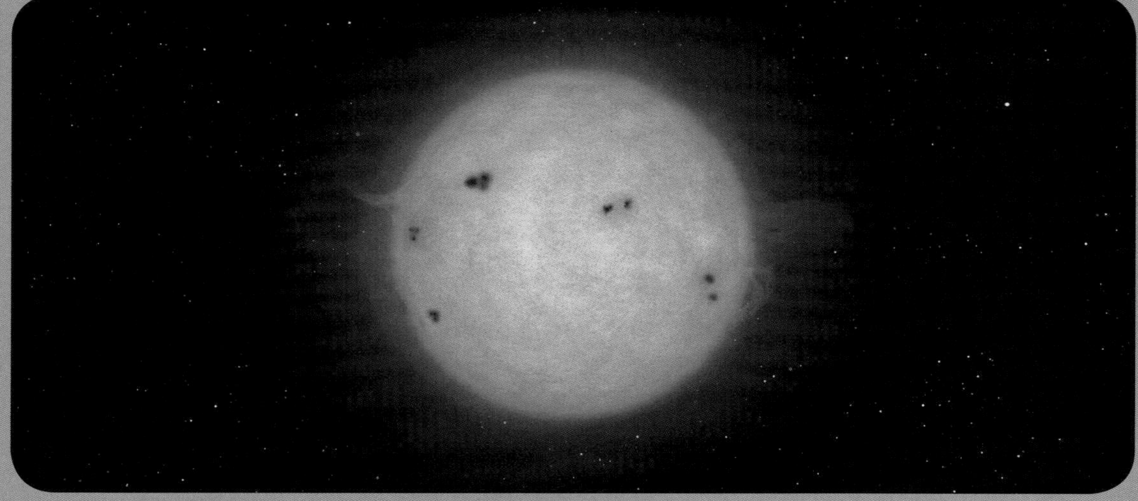

Most stars are red dwarf stars.

Yellow Stars

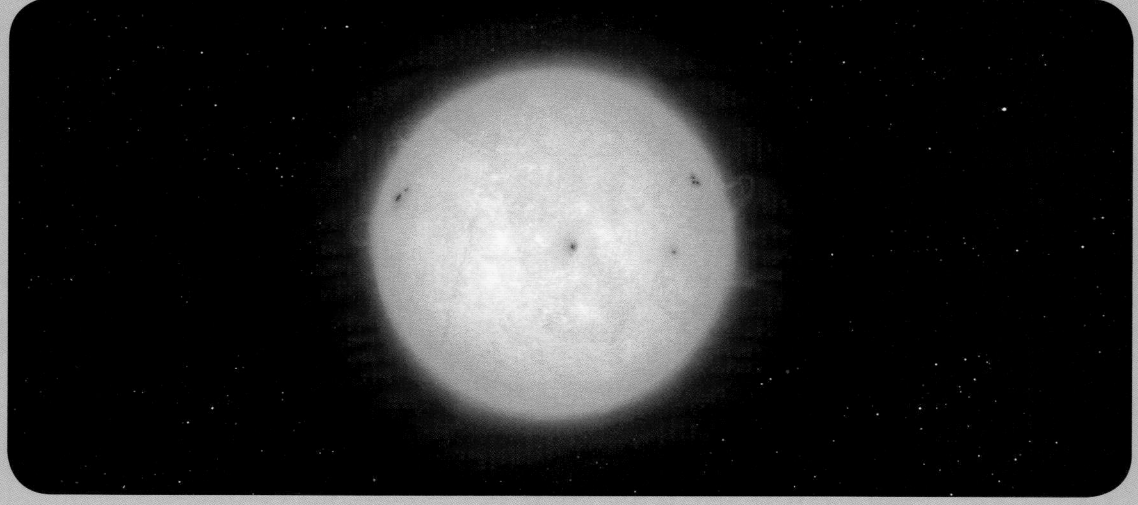

The sun is a yellow star.

Blue Giants

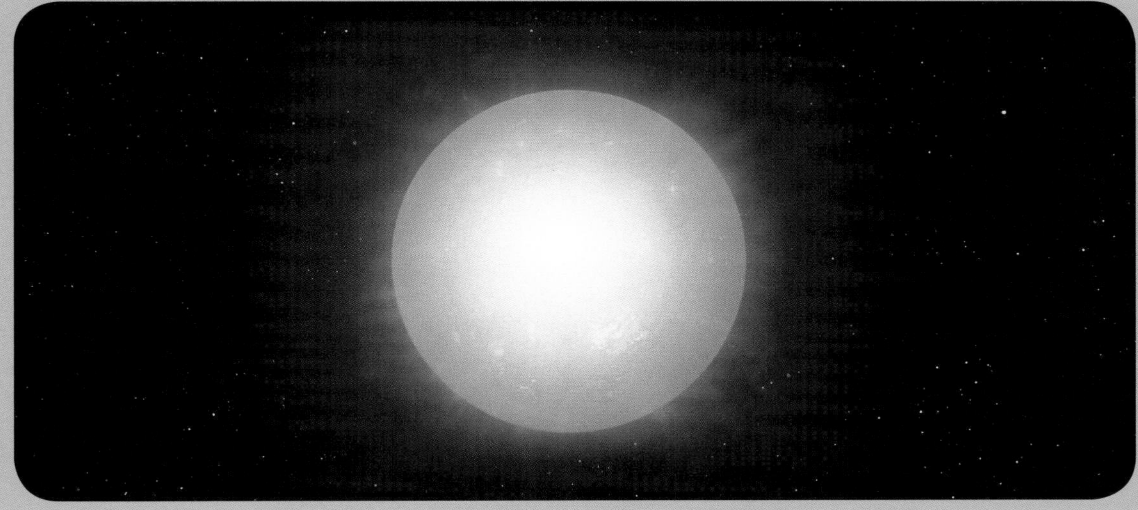

Blue giants are big and very hot.

Supergiants

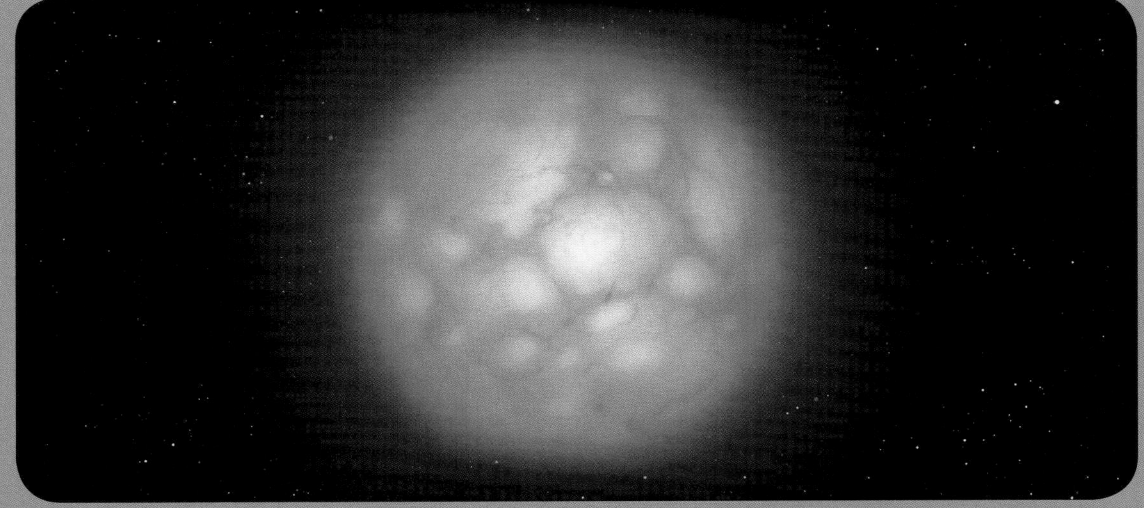

Supergiants are old and very big.

There are lots of stars in the sky.

We cannot go to the stars.
They are too far away.

Patterns in the Sky

People use the stars to find their way.

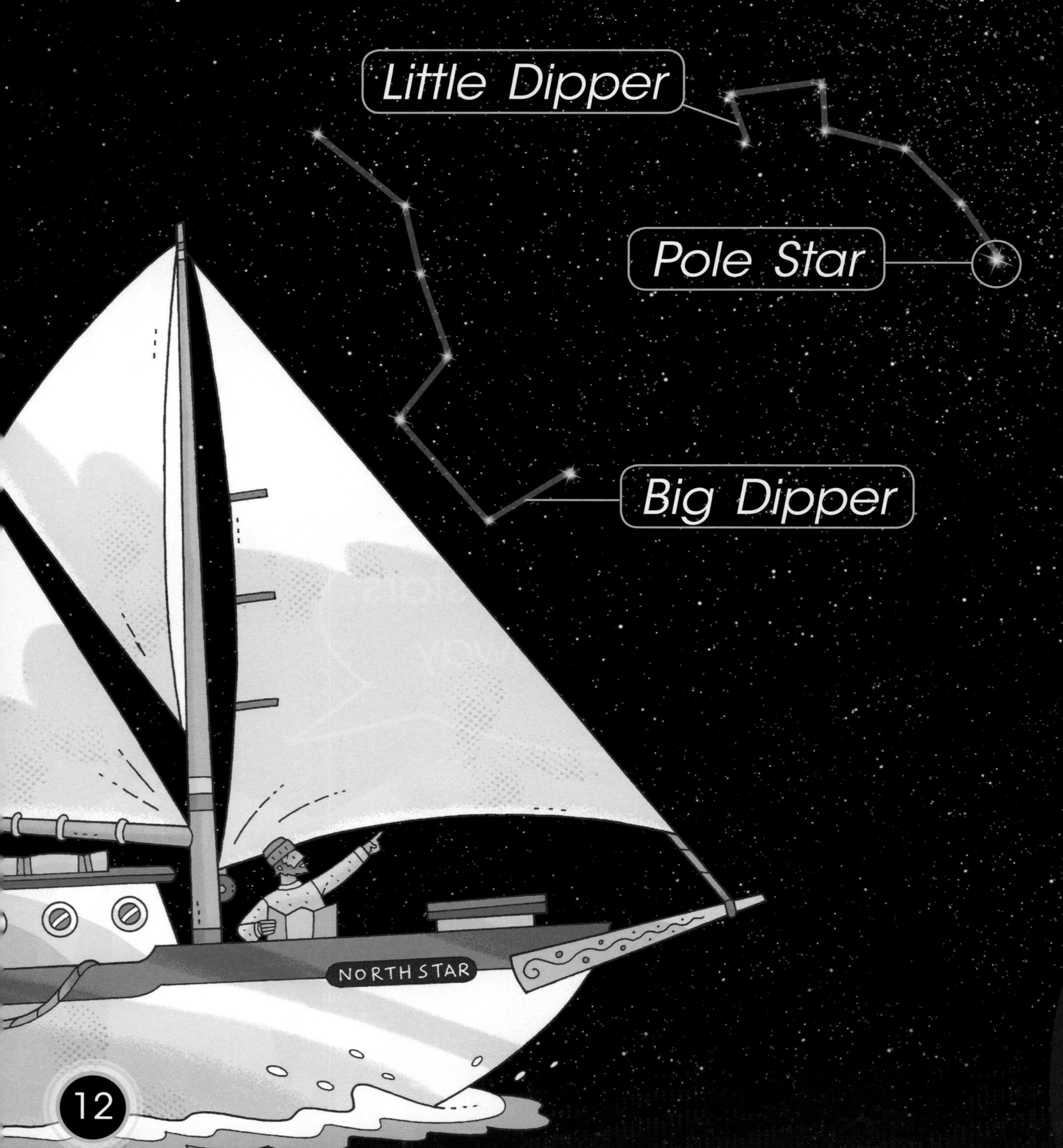

Big Dipper

Southern Cross
Look at
the star **patterns**.

Go outside and look at the sky.

Glossary

dust small bits of something, almost like powder

earth planet that we live on

gas matter that is a bit like air

patterns ways that things are arranged

Stars – Lauri Kubuitsile

Teaching notes written by Sue Bodman and Glen Franklin

Using this book

Developing reading comprehension

This non-chronological report explores facts about stars. It uses the device of an 'expert' scientist to provide information and this serves as a guide through the book for the reader. Simple non-fiction features such as headings, captions and diagrams are included. A glossary supports comprehension of subject-specific vocabulary.

Grammar and sentence structure

- Verb usage is typical of non-fiction reports (*'Stars are …'. 'The sun is …'*).
- Some simple use of causal connectives (*'It looks big because it is close to the earth.'*).
- More variation of sentence structure.

Word meaning and spelling

- The text includes a wide range of known high frequency words (*'is', 'are', 'the', 'in'*) which children can read automatically to support phrased, fluent reading.
- Compound words (*'supergiants', 'outside', 'cannot'*) which can be broken into 'chunks' for reading.
- Some technical vocabulary (*'dust', 'gas'*) can be decoded using phonic knowledge, with contextual meaning gained through the use of the glossary.

Curriculum links

Science – This text will support non-fiction topics on space and space travel. Children could also explore the use of simple telescopes. Exploring perspective (that objects look smaller when they are further away) could be an interesting activity.

Language Development – The book is narrated by a scientific 'expert'. As part of a non-fiction topic, children could assume the role of expert to explain what they have found out about stars. This could form a short video presentation.

Learning Outcomes

Children can:

- track the print with their eyes, finger-pointing only at points of difficulty
- search for information in print to attempt and confirm new words while reading
- make links between this text and other non-fiction texts they have read.

A guided reading lesson

Book Introduction

Begin by discussing what children know already about stars. Give each child a book and read the title to them. Establish this is a non-fiction text by looking at the features and layout.

Orientation

Give a brief overview of the book, using the verb in the continuous present tense form as it is used in the text: *This book tells us what stars are and what they are made from. Stars look very small, don't they? I wonder if they really are – perhaps the book will tell us.*

Preparation

Look the contents page. Draw children's attention to page 4. *This page might be a good place to start. It is going to tell us what a star is. Turn to that page, everyone.* Ask the children to read page 4 quietly to themselves and then ask: *Are stars really small?* Refer the section in the text that explains that they are far away. Ensure accurate decoding of the technical words *'dust'* and *'gas'*, and use the glossary to establish the meaning of these words.

Page 6: It might be difficult for children to understand that the sun is a star which looks big to us because it is nearer the Earth. Demonstrate how things can look smaller when they are far away and bigger when they are nearer, by looking at trees or buildings from the classroom window, perhaps.

Pages 8 and 9: This two-page spread has a different layout. Check the children are able to read across the page, tracking accurately left to right. Draw attention to the compound word *'Supergiants'* on page 9. Demonstrate breaking the word into syllable chunks to read.